A Life Transforming Book

Unlock The Power of Uniqueness

Blueprint for Lifelong Success

Find Your Purpose, Embrace Your True Self,
Build A Magnetic Presence,
and Elevate Your Personal Brand

Jayaprakash Nagathihalli
Transformation Mentor

Dear Reader

You have consistently responded positively to all our books. Many of you have shared how adopting our ideas has helped you reach greater heights in life. Such feedback inspires us to write more. Some of you have also participated in our classes and workshops, buying extra copies to give to others. Salute to you all! Reading will uplift your life. Best wishes to you.

Books in Kannada by Jayaprakash Nagatihalli

1. *Nudigannadi*
2. *Solugalige Anjadiri*
3. *Keelarime Enu? Yeke? Hegge?*
4. *Anukshana Anubhavisi*
5. *Udyoga Kaushalyagalu*
6. *Tiruvugala Arivu*
7. *Ananyate Ariyiri*
8. *Sadhakara Chandana*
9. *Sahitya Chandana*
10. *Vyaktitva Chandana*
11. *Nirupane Nirupisi*
12. *Jeevanotsaha*
13. *Vyaktitwa Darpana*
14. *Vyaktitwa Parivartane*
15. *Lifu Namdene*

Books in English by Jayaprakash Nagatihalli

1. *Fear Not Failures*
2. *Inferiority Complex*
3. *Celebrate Every Moment*
4. *Transform Your Life Instantly*
5. *Unlock the Power of Uniqueness*

With great joy, we present this book to readers who have warmly received our previous works. Many of you have shared valuable feedback via letters, emails, and phone calls, which has further inspired us.

Author's Experience

30 years of recognition in the field of *personality development*. Over 10 lakh people have been trained, and in the past 5 years, we have also reached many people through online classes. Our ideas continue to spread through social media. Seeing some of our trainees emerge as achievers has further fueled our enthusiasm.

Read this book completely and share your feedback. For **Online or Offline training** or guidance, feel free to contact us.

Contact Information:

Bengaluru
Jayaprakash Nagathihalli

Date: 15th January 2025

Mobile: +91 9886081188

Your suggestions and feedback are always welcome:
Office Mobile Numbers: +91 9341259267/ +91 9620303000
Email:smilingjp@gmail.com

Find us on social media:*Jayaprakash Nagathihalli*

YouTube Channels:

1. *Jayaprakash Nagathihalli*
2. *Transformation Unlimited*

Foreword

It is a pleasure to meet all of you through this book. For my 4 English books, you responded very well and that **motivated me** to write this 5th book.

1. Fear Not Failures
2. Inferiority Complex
3. Celebrate Every Moment
4. Transform Your Life Instantly

I have received positive feedback from many people through letters, e-mails and phone calls, which has encouraged my writing. Till now Writing was my 4th priority. Thank you all for the encouragement. My profession is training and guidance and so it becomes my first priority. From now on, my second priority in life will be 'writing'. More books/works can be expected in the coming days. This book/work can transform your life in many ways. Please read it carefully.

Lines from Kuvempu's poem

1. Beat the Kannada drum/damaruga
Lord Shiva the heart of Karnataka
Beat the Kannada drum/damaruga

Or

2. Play the beat of Kannada
Oh Shiva the heart of Karnataka
Play the beat of Kannada

Wake up those who look asleep
Convince and unite the quarrelling crowd
Shed tears over jealousy

And bless them to live together."**Wake up those who look asleep"** These lines of the above poem had a profound effect on me. Our training is also designed with that intention.

"Wake up those who look asleep.

Oh my soul, transcend all boundaries."

- Kuvempu

These are the lines from G.S. Shivarudrappa's poem

I looked for God who is not

In temples made of clay and stones

Not seeing in the love and friendship in us.

We are close, yet miles apart.

In the fortress of our ego,

To accommodate is it that tough

In our life of four-days.

These lines of GSS's about ego, harmony, love, and friendship convey a deep meaning.

"Life is a continuous process of learning," These words of Lal Bahadur Shastri have inspired me to be a student and continue my learning throughout.

"Arise, awake, don't stop till you reach your goal," said Swami Vivekananda.

Why did Vivekananda say, *"Get up first"* Doesn't that mean that most people are sleeping?

Our training, guidance and creation have the following objectives.

1. Scaling Up

2. Enhance

3. Battery Charging

4. Polishing

5. Tuning - Fine Tuning:

6. Positoning Re-Positioning

7. Push

8. Motivation

9. Transformation

10. Be A Real Hero

11. Create Your Own Destiny

12. Script Your Future

13. Small Goals To Big Goals

14. Channelise

15. Beat Yourself

16. Living Larger Than Life

We are working towards– such objectives.

During the course of the work, my friend B.M. Raghavendra has helped me in collecting some information. Sharanu chetti has enhanced the beauty of the book by creating good diagrams.

Seeing that there was not enough information and material available about uniqueness. I am venturing into bringing out this book.

Let your support be there always.

Read, transform, transcend, those who want to participate in training

Contact

Jayaprakash Nagathihalli
Mob: 9886081188

Your suggestions are always welcome.

Mobile numbers: 9341259267 and 9620303000
e-mail: smilingjp@gmail.com

Search on social media: JayaprakashNagathihalliYouTube
Channels:
1. Jayaprakash Nagathihalli
2. Transformation Unlimited

Gratitude

I would like to express my gratitude to <u>Sooraj Achar</u>, B.V. Venkatshyam, Santosh Chandrashekhar Hulagabali, T.G. Shivaraj, Basavaraj Mudbagil, Anjali & Impu Jayaprakash who have helped me in finalising the Book at different levels.

I thank Sharanu Chetty who has done Artworks for this entire book

Contents

1.

UNIQUENESS

Everyone in the world is unique. But how many people are aware of their uniqueness? This is a tricky question.

If everyone is aware of their uniqueness, there is no doubt that it will contribute to building a beautiful society.

Realization of uniqueness,makes the person self-aware.

Self-awareness leads to the recognition of capabilities.

It helps the talents to bloom. It is difficult to achieve this without effort.

Awareness of weaknesses is also important.

We should recognize our weaknesses and get control over them. Our focus should be on acquiring the needed knowledge, skills and practices.

A positive attitude also plays an important role. There was no one like us before; there is no one like us today; there will be no one like us in the future; that is, we are all unique, not just a replica of anyone.. Making good use of the good opportunities that come to us also contributes to the changes in our lives.

Being Aware of such turning points is important.To know more about Awareness of turns (buy and read the book 'Awareness of Turns' by the same author which is available at Sapna Bookhouse).

It is common to encounter setbacks while moving forward in any field.

One should face such situations with confidence.

The above ideas are identified as SWOT Analysis.

Identifying Strengths, Weakness, Opportunities and Threats is SWOT. These Ideas help everyone understand themselves better. When each one of us adopt our own lifestyle, then one can clearly see the uniqueness of such individuals.

The English film 'Catch Me If You Can' is based on a real story. It is about a fraudster who is taken into confidence and given responsibility. In the movie Frank Abaglale is an expert at writing bank checks and forging them. His crimes are discovered and he is sent to prison. An investigating officer recognizes his expertise in forgery. He recommends that the banks can use his expertise to detect other criminals. This advice is put into practice. He is given the position of bank officer. He saves the banks from incurring losses.

Imperfections make us Special.

Our Imperfections make us Special. We should be aware of that and move forward.

Everyone should understand that no one is perfect. "My choices are like my finger prints they make me unique- says Deepika Padukone.

That means we have to make good choices in many situations that come up in our lives. Listen to your inner voice. To understand your passions, love and desires listen to your inner voice. You will get the answers you need. Questions will arise, and with them you will find the answers there only.

Your Uniqueness is what makes you special and that is beautiful.- NIA JAX

Always remember that you are absolutely unique. Just like everyone else.-Margaret Mead

What can we do to realize our uniqueness?

1. UPDATE- To make it happen today, Our thoughts and actions need to complement current events and developments.

2. UPGRADE– Along with today's development
Thinking ahead and being proactive will help us take another step forward.

3. RE-INVENT- Re-inventing ourselves is essential for progress.

4. BEST VERSION- Just as we are constantly striving for the best version of technology like mobile, we need to recognize the best version of ourselves.

5. SELF-AWARENESS- Self-awareness is the ability to make our talents bloom better through continuous awareness and understanding.

A Clear Vision of Life inoculates you from distractions

A clear vision of our life keeps us away from unnecessary thoughts. Thus, the more our awareness becomes clear, the more beautiful dimensions of life are revealed.

You are the masterpiece of your life. It is very important to know that you are the masterpiece of your life.

The Last Supper by the famous artist Leonardo da Vinci is his masterpiece. Mona Lisa is also another of his Art work.

- Don't compare

- Don't ever compare anyone

- Each one is different from another

- The sun is different from the moon

- If the sun is hot and bright, the moon is cool yet throws light

- All are important here

- Nobody is useless

- Don't compare your progress with that of others. We all need our own time to travel our own distance.

- Don't compare your progress to that of others.We all need our own time to travel our own distance.

- Our life journey is our own. Don't compare yourself with others.

- Autographs and photographs become the measure of your success.

- The moment your signature becomes an autograph, it can be called the beginning of your success. This is a good measure of your achievement.

Photograph

In recent days, more and more people like to take photographs. They consider the moment as a beautiful moment.

Selfie

Most people are addicted to selfies due to the rise of mobile phones.

Know your Own Strength

You are a force. That force is within you. Intelligence, knowledge, skills help bring out the deep talent within you.

"Your uniqueness is your magic."

2.

LIFE IS BEAUTIFUL

400 years ago, Purandaradasa warned the mankind- 'Human life is great, don't waste it, you crazy people…'. 'Many become part of geography; Only few make history' The sentence seems to be asking us which group we like to join? 'Though born poor? Death should be history' should be our wish.

Lines of a small poem of Sri. Jaraganahalli Shivashankar's poem is as follows:

A tree that stood as a shade for ten years

Remained as a beam for hundreds of years

A king who ruled for a hundred years

Did not remain as a corpse even for three days

The above four lines convey a mystical message

Man wants the soil

Soil wants the man

Finally, it is soil, that wins not the man

When a person is young, they offer fruit

When he grows up, they offer him a woman

When he dies, they offer mud"

This is what life is all about

"Others gave birth,

others gave name,

others gave education,

others gave income,

others gave honour,

others gave the first and last bath

after you - others will get your property,

others will perform your funeral."

"Horoscope at birth

Sutak (mourning) at death

Dram In between

This is life"

Just change the words; life changes.

A blind man will be asking for help holding a placard that says, "I am blind please help." But most people don't respond. A young woman notices this and changes the letters on the placard.

"Today is a beautiful day. But I can't see it."

Everyone who notices this sign donates him money. Even though the meaning of both sentences is the same, the feeling they convey is different, words have such an impressive power. Realize that contextual word usage has magical power.

Importance Of Today

- Today is an auspicious day

- This week is an auspicious week

- Today's star is an auspicious star,

- Today's yoga is an auspicious yoga,

"Today's ascendant (lagna) is an auspicious ascendant"

- Purandaradasaru

Think and plan in the morning; review all those ideas in the evening.

'Today' is a beautiful opportunity between tomorrow's beliefs and yesterday's mistakes.

"Yesterday is past, tomorrow is future, why should we worry about them today?" This song from a movie also conveys a good message.

Actor and director Shankar Nag used to say, It is good to increase the time you are awake because there is more time to sleep after death.

If you manage today properly, your life will be yours.

"Don't waste the day"

–Kumara vyas

Assumption of a beautiful day

Presume every day as a beautiful day. Think like that and live like that.

Let's us get into the practice of telling ourselves "It is a Beautiful morning, Beautiful afternoon, beautiful evening, Beautiful good night" every day and make every day beautiful.

Greetings (Namaskara)

Starting the meeting by exchanging greetings makes a good beginning.
It is a great way of respecting others. It can have a great impact throughout (all the 24-hours) the day.
Happiness

Always keep smiling and be happy. Let your mind be inclined only towards positive thoughts. A happy mental state can keep us away from many diseases.

These three lines of D.R. Bendre describe life beautifully:

Happiness is birth

Hostiity is death

Harmony is life

"One should not devour another person and live; one should understand the other and live."

-D.R. Bendre

3.

MINDSET OF ACCEPTANCE

Brooding over the things that you have not got, do not forget what you have
In the midst of adversity Count your blessings

"This is a way to happiness" - **mankutimma**

Brooding over the things that you have not got, do not forget what you have
In the midst of adversity Count your blessings
Don't bother about the things that are out of your reach. Just count your blessings and enjoy the fortune that is in your hands with satisfaction. This is the path to joy, to happiness, to true happiness.

Benefits of Satsangh

"The company of good people is sweet like honey
The company of bad people is like getting bitten by
honeybees."

- Sarvajna

Our personality is often measured by who we associate with and what books we read. Choosing the right people is the key to success in life.

It is better to fight (rub) with sandalwood than to play with dung.

Even if you have to fight, fight with the good - These words warn us to stay away from the bad people.

It is better to quarrel with wise people than to be friends with ignorant people.–Kanakadasa

The smell of jasmine flower-

This is a parable told by Ramakrishna Paramahamsa.

An occasion arises when a fisher woman had to sleep in the house of a jasmine seller. She finds it hard to sleep because of the smell of jasmine flowers. She explains this to the lady of the house, takes the fish basket, keeps it by her side and happily goes off to sleep. We love the things we like the most.

A situation apt for the mood

It is said that becoming a successful person and wealthy starts with the mindset. If the mindset is understood properly, and anybody who understand the perspective of positivity end up as happy people.

A tiny rope tied to the elephant's leg.

An iron chain will be tied to the leg of the elephant calf and made to believe that it cannot free itself from the chain. The baby elephant feels that no matter what is tied to its leg, it cannot be untied. It behaves in the same way. Even when the elephant grows up, it does not make any effort to free itself even if a small rope is tied to it.

Similarly, many people never come out of their past experiences. Only those who try to come out become successful people.

Just as you celebrate victory, accept defeat with humility. No success is final, nor is defeat the end. Life is the courage to move forward, balancing both.

Buy and read the book 'FEAR NOT FAILURES' written by Jayaprakash Nagathihalli It is available at Sapna Bookhouse.

Life is not a bed of flowers

It is not possible for only good things to happen to us always. Develop the mindset to look at both hardships and pleasures the same way.

Sachin Tendulkar, who is called the God of Cricket, did not excel in the tenth grade. But now there is a lesson about him in the tenth grade textbook. ~

Bill Gates is not a graduate. But he has hired rank holders from leading universities around the world to work for his Microsoft company.

Do whatever you can, don't say I'm just a piece of straw

In this world temple no work is inferior, you have a place here.

Do whatever job you can. Don't say, 'I am a mere human being, Is it possible for me to do anything?'. In this World temple, no work is insignificant. You too have the opportunity to do some work, to do something, and to tell the truth that everything created in the world has a use.

Sometimes you have to eat your words, chew your ego, Swallow your pride and accept that you are wrong. It is not giving up. It is called growing up.

"The whole world is a treasure trove of delicacies for those who know the Accepting mindset"

- G. S. Shivarudrappa

4.

ATTITUDE OF GRATITUDE

Gratitude is the key to happiness; Happiness is the key to success.

Those who are grateful feel happy.

It also helps in maintaining the mental balance. It gives hope about life.

Gratitude brings everyone together. It gives us a feeling of being with others and also a satisfied feeling that we are better than we are.

Gratitude produces happy hormones in our body. This leads to good health. It is very beneficial for both the giver and the recipient, it also increases the bonding amongst individuals. The experience of supreme happiness is also achieved. Most importantly, it helps in changing the personality. This gradually becomes a part of our personality.

The word GRATITUDE is derived from the Latin word GRATUS Dow, meaning "to be grateful or thankful." It is also recognised as a positive response of kindness. It is also a 'blessing' of positive attitudes, actions, and thoughts.

Nature

We have to remember Mother Nature. Nature has helped us in many ways to sustain our lives through the five elements.

Earth Day

We must pay respect to the earth on which we are living Although Earth Day is celebrated symbolically for one day, every day should be treated with respect.

Environment Day

It is everyone's responsibility to maintain a beautiful and clean environment. Let's understand the meaning of the sentence Cleanliness is next to Godliness.

Parents

Parents are the Living gods to us, it is everyone's primary duty to treat them with due respect.
Do not send them to old age homes except in unavoidable circumstances.

Pitru Paksha

Pitru Paksha is a great tradition in our culture. It is a tradition of paying respect to every member of the family of the past generations.

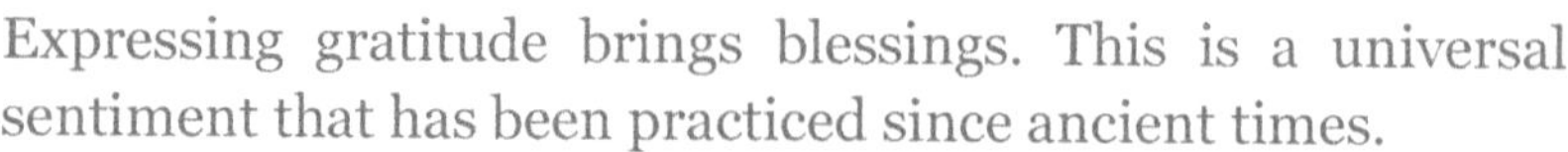

Expressing gratitude brings blessings. This is a universal sentiment that has been practiced since ancient times.

Praying with a feeling of gratitude brings in a magical effect.

Gurus/Mentors/Teachers- From ignorance to wisdom (bliss)

No matter what profession individuals choose, it is the teachers and lecturers who shape them. As teachers, they find joy in the progress of their students. It is our duty to respect and express gratitude to such people.

-A study from Harvard University shows that gratitude leads to more happiness.

Guru's guidance makes us know the joy of gratitude

To those who helped and resolved the problem

In this long journey of our life, there are umpteen number of people who have stood by us and helped with our problems. When such people are in need of any support, helping them becomes important. Exchanging greetings, gifts, giving financial support, and giving them some time will add grace to your personality. Inculcating a bit of gratitude in our attitude has an amazing impact on the temperament.

Well-wishers

We are blessed with well-wishers in many ways and forms. It is also equally important to watch and recognize such people. Interacting with well-wishers is a solace to the mind. They fill your life with enthusiasm.

For those who have shown humanity

-We should be grateful to all those who serve the society. Whether we know them personally or not, it should be our duty to pay tribute to true volunteers.

Uniqueness

You should be unique
To prosper in your life you only have to sweat it out.
To be away from inferiority superiority complexes
Brooding is poison, showing off is poison

Leave the Illusion I
Feel you are one amongst others
For the excellence of Society
Be humane
So be unique

Uniqueness is you being yourself
Muddunanda
(Online student Yogananda)

Ways to express gratitude
You can show respect in any way you feel like. The feeling behind is important here. Saying Thank You Is very important here. You can show respect by bowing to elders. You can give a flower bouquet. You can give them good books. You can even convey your gratitude through a smile. You can remember, express and appreciate their support in front of people.

Debt (runa) repayment to invisible hands

Don't know the grain from your plate goes to which water stream and sprouts in which soil I the food from that is for the world II Who can explain this?- mankutimma

When you wash the plate you ate on, the food left on it mixes with the water and enters which stream. Where does it land and mix with the soil and grow into a plant? Who will eat the rice that comes from it? What benefit will the world get from eating that rice? Who will explain this?

If I am able to live happily in this world, it is not only because of me. Many people, from many places, through their toil have contributed towards our happiness. We owe every moment of our joy to thousands of those invisible hands.

Gratitude is the mother root of evolution.
There is a feeling that gratitude is on the decline in recent times. However, we need not be completely disheartened. You can see this feeling in at least some people.

When you move your focus from COMPETITION TO CONTRIBUTION life becomes celebration.

If we look at our present situation and if we become aware of that situation, we will start to feel grateful for this life.

There is no doubt that the world, country, nature, family, and friends contribute in making our lives beautiful. In return the only gift we are able to give back is Gratitude.

Response in animals and birds.

The dog is a grateful animal. Ant is known for its discipline. Donkey is a testament to hard work. Every animal and bird have its own unique characteristics. There are many examples of humans establishing relationships with wild animals as well. Animals and birds contribute to our well-being. Let us love and respect such animals.

Barack Obama

I had watched some videos of Barack Obama during his tenure as the President of the United States. I noticed him thanking the pilot and security officer of the plane he was on. The scenes where he would mix with children were eye-catching. He would always serve the guests at dinner parties. Those scenes always made me feel that everyone should be like him.

We all should remember farmers while eating and soldiers while sleeping.

Know 'uniqueness'

Soldiers

Our soldiers are the ones who are risking their lives to protect us. A salute to the soldiers who work with dedication, putting aside their desires and aspirations.

Farmers:

Farmers must grow crops to quench our hunger. Nothing can match a farmers' hard work. The author takes pride in being born in a farmers' family.

Let us bow to the Negila yogis./plow men

The annual program of Nagamma Foundation is named Gratitude

The author is involved in social activities through a trust named after his mother Nagamma.

The tradition of honouring known and unknown individuals who have contributed to the society is held every year in the month of September. Those who have been honoured here have received national awards like Padma Shri and doctorates. Every year, we witness heart warming moments of this model program. Instead of cutting a cake this is how this author celebrates his birthday

JP with, Padma Shri Recipient Harekala Hajabba,

Grazing in some place, drinking water elsewhere II
Who drinks the milk it produces II. And the world benefits
from that in what way, nobody knows II Ponder over this
movement of Runa/debt.–mankutimma

A cow grazes grass in some place, drinks water elsewhere, and
gives milk. Someone drinks that milk? By drinking it what
power he gets? Who knows what benefit the world derives
from the power that comes to those who drink milk? Ponder
over this movement of Runa/debt.

'Inhale Love; Exhale Gratitude'

May your life flourish through gratitude

5.

LOVE WHO YOU ARE BECOME WHO YOU ARE - LIVE WHO YOU ARE

"To fall in love with yourself is the first secret to happiness."

-Robert Morley

Recognize Your Physical and Inner Beauty

The shape of our body we are born with is not in our hands. We must accept our present looks and work to shape our body the way we desire. There are countless ways to exercise. The field of makeup has grown tremendously. The choices in clothing and attire have increased.

It is up to you to take the initiative to fulfill your desires and aspirations.

Inner beauty depends on your state of mind.

Your thought processes have a profound impact.

By controlling your mind and focusing on priorities with proper planning, success is assured.

Wear the outfits you like

Instead of focusing on how expensive the clothes are, focus on how well their colours and styles suit you. There have been revolutionary changes in clothing design. Set aside some time for yourself. Take advice from friends and family. Dress well; clean and elegant clothing will bring you joy.

My song is my own.
My melody is my own.
My rhythm is my own.
My aspirations are my own.

Wherever I go, I will forever
Remain true to myself.
I will speak, I will act,
I will strive —
This is my life

The cloud to the blue sky,
The clouds filled with beauty
The bird fly and soared high
Calmly and joyfully

A cool breeze is blowing
The river's water is flowing
The green grass has spread like a soft bed
Flowers are blooming on the vine
The beauty of the world feels like it's all mine

Even if a hundred people come
Even if a hundred people go
I am my own companion
Forever a joyful soul, I know

Even if it is scorching hot
Even if the thunderstorm pours down
For me, it's all joy
For you, it's a new perspective
Day and night are beautiful, aren't they?

Every line of this song composed by Ch. Udayashankar is
worth pondering and following.

A Foreigner's Reflection at Kudle Beach

This is an incident shared with us by the kind-hearted Rajeev Gaonkar. A man who had been living alone for six months at Kudle Beach in Gokarna was asked if he ever felt lonely staying there all by himself. His response was, "How am I alone? I have the sea, the rocky cliffs, the fish, animals, birds, the beautiful sky, the locals, and the travellers with me."

If we change the way we think, everything else will change.

Achiever Angela Merkel:

Dr. J.S. Patil shared a piece of information on social media about Angela Merkel, a remarkable achiever who lived life her way.

Germany Bids Farewell to Angela Merkel with Blessings:

The streets of Germany, balconies of homes, and windows across the nation resonated with six minutes of warm applause to honor Angela Merkel. This was truly unique—an exceptional moment worth understanding. An unforgettable moment that honoured leadership and a personality that safeguarded humanity.

The Germans chose her to lead the nation.

She led 80 million Germans continuously for 18 years with her extraordinary ability, exceptional skills, unique dedication, and unmatched integrity. She never spoke nonsense. She was never seen on the streets of Berlin for a photograph. The world called her "The Lady of the World" and recognized her as equal to six million men.

During her eighteen years in power, no cases of legal violations were registered against her. She did not appoint any of her relatives to government positions. She did not claim to establish the greatest glory in the country. She did not accept lakhs of rupees as a salary for serving the country. She did not criticize those who were in power before her. Today, Germany and its people are in a better position across all fronts.

On the day of her retirement, the reaction of Germans was unprecedented in the history of the country. The entire nation stood on their balconies and applauded spontaneously for six minutes. The people of the country gave her a nationwide standing ovation.

Germany bid an unforgettable farewell to its leader, a chemical physicist who did not succumb to the allure of fashion, the glow of the limelight, or the temptation of real estate. She did not desire new cars, yachts, or private planes.

At a press conference, a journalist asked her: "We've noticed you wear the same suit. Don't you have any other suits?"

To which she replied, "I am a government employee, not a model who acts in advertisements."

Another question was: Do you have housekeepers who clean your house and prepare your meals? Answer: No, I don't have servants and I don't need them. My husband and I do all the work at home every day.

Mrs Merkel lives in an ordinary apartment like any other citizen. She lived in the same place before her election and even after becoming Chancellor, but she did not like the Bungalows, servants, swimming pools or gardens. Mrs Merkel, the former chancellor of Germany, now Europe's largest economy.

"This is a great example of enlightening, raising awareness and educating the people of our country."

Self Image

Self-image is the way you think and see yourself. It helps you to understand your inner self.

This process will help you gain a clear understanding of yourself. Identify your physical, mental, intellectual, emotional, spiritual, and financial aspects.

You are what you are.

You become what you feel. You become what you think.

Clarity in thoughts emerges based on your ability to perceive. These thoughts eventually shape into actions. Your thoughts and actions are what others recognize as your personality. If you dream of a life that aligns with who you truly are and move toward your goals, clarity is achieved. Overall, remember that society identifies you as an individual. However, it is better to recognize yourself before society does.

Avoid Comparisons.

Unnecessary comparisons are not needed. There is no need to compare yourself with others. Similarly, it is important to ensure that others do not interfere in your life. Do not meddle in others' problems, but also do not let those who interfere in your matters go unchecked. Many problems can be resolved through effective communication skills. Maintain self-confidence and face situations with courage.

"Respect means so many things to so many people.

To some it is everything."

- Sangeetha Rana

6.

FIRE YOUR PASSION

"The only way to do great work is to love what you do."

— **Steve Jobs**

Where there is a will, there is a way; Where there is a goal, there is success (there is heaven)

It is always better to make our passions our goals. Instead of digging multiple pits in different places, it is wise to dig deep in one place. Without a goal, our life has no direction or clarity. We realize the true purpose of life only when we have clear goals. When we focus our mind and direct it towards our passionate goals, the right path becomes visible.

Reasons why many do not set goals:

1.   Pessimistic mindset
2.   Fear of failures
3.   Lack of awareness about the importance of goals
4.   Lack of knowledge on goal setting
5.   Absence of ambition
6.   Low self-esteem
7.   Fear of rejection

Reasons for goal failure:

1.   Not having a true goal
2.   Not writing down the goal
3.   Lack of accountability
4.   Absence of rewards or results
5.   No specific time frame
6.   Constantly changing goals

Ask yourself: What do you want? What is your plan to achieve it? What are your efforts? These questions will help you stay on track with your goals. Every day, every week, every month, and every year, you should review your goals. That is why writing down your goals is always beneficial. Goals enhance your motivation and productivity. As you see progress, you will experience excitement.

Why are goals important?

1. To take control of your life
2. To focus on key matters
3. To make better decisions
4. To complete tasks effectively
5. To build self-confidence
6. To progress towards growth and success

Types of Goals:

1. Short-term
2. Mid-term
3. Long-term

Ask yourself three questions:

1. What do I want to achieve?
2. Why do I want to achieve it?
3. How will I achieve it?

Key areas where goals should be set:

1. Family
2. Financial
3. Attitude
4. Education

5. Happiness
6. Social Service
7. Career
8. Physical Health
9. Spiritual Growth

"Turn dreams into goals, and always aim for your goals."

*"A dream is just a dream, but a goal is
a dream with a plan and a deadline."*

*"The difference between an ordinary person and a great
person lies in the degree of concentration."*

— Swami Vivekananda

*"If you truly love what you do, the work becomes easy, and
its purpose is almost fulfilled."*

-Mark Zuckerberg

7.

BEING DIFFERENT

"Different is good, and being different is what makes us stand out in the world."

— Natalya Neidhart

Who am I?

Ramana

Spiritual gurus like the sages (Maharshis) and Sri Ramakrishna Paramahamsa have taught that one should frequently ask this question. There is a profound message hidden within this question. If asked repeatedly in different situations and at different stages of life, it awakens self-awareness and helps in discovering the purpose of life.

Anthropology

Anthropology has proven that physical differences exist according to natural regions. In India, one can notice variations in language, behaviour, clothing, customs, and traditions every 50 kilometers.

Unity in Diversity

India is a country that has achieved unity in diversity. Travelling across India feels like travelling through a miniature world. The natural wealth of India, comparable to many international destinations, is a source of pride.

Excellence in Diversity–Sharanu Chetty

Throughout this book, artist Sharanu Chetty's illustrations are present. He is recognized as a teacher, writer, and cartoonist. Despite not having physical growth like others, he has proven through his talent that he is in no way inferior to anyone.

A conversation with Sharanu Chetty:

How did you adapt to being physically different?

I am from Golageri village in Sindagi Taluk, Vijayapura District. My father, Gollalappa, and mother, Gangabai, had five daughters before I was born. However, my growth was normal like others. Due to stunted physical growth, I used to feel sad during my childhood days. I was troubled by the fact that I did not grow tall like others. People made fun of my physical appearance and used to make sarcastic remarks. The hobbies I cultivated during childhood helped me forget my pain. In the fifth grade, I started drawing. I also wrote and sang self-composed songs at school events. By the time I reached college, I had developed a strong grasp of painting, singing, literature, and writing. Some people appreciated my talent, while others criticized it. I accepted all reactions equally. Observing cartoons in newspapers, I shifted my focus towards cartoon drawing. Some people, out of jealousy, made negative comments about my drawings. The same happened with my singing and writing. However, I did not let it bother me and continued forward. My father, mother, family, and close friends stood by me. Through persistent practice, I earned recognition as a cartoonist. I even published a book titled *Tuntamakkalu* (Naughty Kids).

I also had a dream of becoming a teacher. However, people tried to discourage me by saying,

"You are not fit to be a teacher. You won't be able to reach the blackboard. Children as tall as you will not respect you. You lack the ability to be a teacher."

Ignoring Negative Words, Rising to Success

I did not pay any attention to the negative comments. I just pursued teacher training and secured first place in the training center. Revered Dr. Prabhusarangadeva Shivacharya of Sarangimath, Sindagi, recognized my talent in music, literature, arts, and education, blessed me, and supported me as a mentor. Later, Sri N.M. Biradar, the director of Chanakya Career Academy in Vijayapura, identified my potential, inspired me, and encouraged me to achieve greater heights. Under the guidance of my mentors and through continuous study, I was appointed as a government school teacher. Currently, I am serving at the Government Higher Primary school for Girls in my hometown. To nurture my talent and that of my students, I have established Nudichitra

Publications. Ironically, those who once deemed me unfit to be a teacher later honoured me! With self-confidence, I became a teacher by profession, a cartoonist, writer, and singer by passion. My profession and hobbies have brought me both national and state awards. Vishweshwara Bhatt gave me an opportunity to create daily cartoons for *Vishwavani* newspaper, making my work popular. I have also illustrated books for renowned authors. The Kannada Manikya Monthly Magazine, under the leadership of Veerakaputra Srinivasand Malavalli Prasanna, created an opportunity for me to write children's comics, giving wings to my new dreams. Editors of various newspapers have also encouraged me. I have realized that the insults faced in life often become reasons for future recognition. As an ordinary man, I have accomplished things beyond expectations. What was once now it has almost become a habit for me to achieve the impossible. I have drawn inspiration from many personality development trainers and authors. Your Book like *Solugalige Anjadiri* (FEAR NOT FAILURES) have taught me life lessons and helped me understand different stages of personal growth. Thus, my life so far has been unique. By being active in the media and expressing my talents on appropriate platforms, I have carved a distinct identity. I have embraced my physical appearance and made it attractive.

As Shankar Nag once said:

"You will definitely sleep after you die; achieve something while you are alive!"

These words constantly motivate me to strive for success. I have numerous dream projects in art, literature, and education, and I am actively working towards realizing them.

What is your opinion on uniqueness?

All living beings in this creation are unique. Even a tiny ant can frighten a giant elephant. Despite differences in size, shape, and strength, both the elephant and the ant are unique in their own way. Similarly, we humans are also different from one another. Every individual possesses special skills and abilities. Recognizing and understanding our **inner potential** is the first step towards realizing our uniqueness. Being unique is not about being rich or poor, beautiful or unattractive; rather, it is about having an active and creative personality. Many of us sing like the original singer or even better, but we never consider ourselvessingers. We dance well for fun but never call ourselves dancers. If we overcome this mindset and believe in our capabilities, we become unique! Just as every flower has a distinct fragrance, every person has a unique essence.

Your suggestions on Embracing Uniqueness

> Do not lose your individuality–Embrace yourself as you are. Your appearance or physical condition should not limit your achievements–Disabilities should never be seen as a curse. Avoid comparing yourself with others–Instead create your own identity in what you love. Be the hero of your life–Utilize every moment wisely to achieve success. Many people come into our lives for a reason. Respect those who helped you

grow–Never forget those who supported your journey. Take action immediately–Procrastination hinders uniqueness; taking prompt action enhances personality. Our name should be our best brand–Aim to create a lasting impact through your achievements.

As the saying goes:

"When you were born, you cried while the world laughed; live a life so meaningful that when you leave, the world cries while you smile!" Doesn't this remind us that every one of us is a masterpiece meant to live a fulfilling life?

8.

BE ORIGINAL

BEING ORIGINAL

Be Yourself–know yourself first,

"Don't blindly imitate others just because they seem great."

— **Beechi**

Our originality sets the boundaries to understand the purpose of our life.

A lamp is recognized by its bright light, not by who lit it. Similarly, we must be recognized for our abilities. Birth is not important; the way we live matters. A lotus, though born in the mud, is worthy of worship, whereas a thorny weed, even if found on a mountain, is not worshipped.

Originality is the foundation of success. Do not waste time and energy trying to copy others.

An ignorant person focuses on others' roles, but a wise person focuses on his own. Those who stand on their own feet never fear falling.

Self-respect holds great power. People with purpose, goals, and vision do not have time for drama. They invest their energy in creativity and focus on a positive life. In reality, they truly live.

Understand your own strengths,
Analyze your own qualities,
Observe situations keenly and respond accordingly
Do not exceed your limits unnecessarily
— That is the fortune of the blessed one

–Mankuthimma.

Before starting anything, first ask yourself: Do I have the strength for this? What qualities do I possess for this task? By understanding these and considering the circumstances, if we work within our responsibilities with courage, success will be ours. That is the fortune of the blessed.

I must not be stagnant water; I must be a flowing, sacred stream.

Flowing water is always pure,

A sacred stream is always divine,

Divinity is blended within it.

– B.M. Raghavendra

"To be yourself in a world that is constantly trying to make you something else is the greatest accomplishment."

–Ralph Waldo Emerson

"If you are always trying to be normal, you will never know how amazing you can be."

–Maya Angelou

Rise Above Inferiority complex

We should never think of ourselves as lesser than others.

We must avoid unnecessary comparisons.

As we develop self-confidence, inferiority complex naturally fades away.

What is inferiority complex? Why does it exist? How does it manifest?

The author explores these questions in detail in the book.

Inferiority Complex

True character earns respect; mere acting does not. –B. M. Raghavendra

9.

PERSPECTIVE IS THE LADDER OF LIFE

PERCEPTION

"Ask, and it will be given to you.
Seek, and you will find.
Knock, and the door will be opened for you."

— **The Bible**

Our understanding of life depends on how we perceive things. There may be situations where our thoughts form the very foundation of our experiences.

When perspective changes, the vision changes.

If we bring about a shift in our way of looking at things, we can also notice differences in the outcomes. When we adopt a positive outlook as our standard, the world around us becomes positive. Be aware of the negative, but embrace the positive.

1. Uniqueness means being unparalleled, exceptional, incomparable, and beyond imagination. It is something unprecedented, limitless, and beyond conventional comparison

2. Transcending the extraordinary is what defines uniqueness

3. Understanding the traits, behaviour, beliefs, thinking, and personality of an individual in a specific field by comparing them with another person in the same domain

4. Priorities must be identified and adapted accordingly

5. A collection of small, continuous efforts to enhance awareness

6. The inextricable connection of human qualities and natures, the confluence of human values

7. Diversity is the essence of life's vibrancy

8. A strong, unwavering desire to pursue what one truly wants

9. Curiosity is essential for knowledge enhancement

10. Recognizing that life exists in the present moment and striving for fulfillment

11. Listening to one's inner voice

12. Constantly increasing self-awareness

13. One should show dedication to self-reflection in the journey of leading a meaningful life

14. Whatever one loses, they gain something even greater in return

15. Old age should not be allowed to take over. One should not give it a chance. Stay active without limiting yourself by age. Believe in the philosophy that "doing nothing brings exhaustion, being active you will live longer."

16. Spend the present wisely, with the goal of making the future beautiful. Live by the principle: "Yesterday is old, tomorrow is a dream, today is the reality."

17. To teach, one must learn; to learn, one must teach

18. When today's efforts are utilized wisely, "I must achieve" turns into "I will achieve."

19. Discipline nurtures discipline; one must be a soldier of discipline

"I do not complain to God."

When Arthur Ashe was asked, *"Why don't you complain to God for giving you AIDS?"*, his response was an eye-opener for everyone.

He said,

"In the whole world, millions play tennis, and every tennis player dreams of becoming a Wimbledon Champion. When I became the Wimbledon Champion, I never asked God, 'Why did you make me a Wimbledon Champion?' So now, why should I ask Him, 'Why did you give me AIDS?"

-Arthur Ashe

Arthur Ashe

Factors That Influence Our Thinking

Environment

- The surroundings we live in impact each individual in different ways. What kind of atmosphere do we live in? What kind of people surround us? These factors are crucial.

Education

- We have all observed that those who take education seriously often progress in life. Education helps in shaping lives and guiding people on the right path. Those who fail to recognize the positive aspects of education tend to lag behind.

Experience

- Life experiences help in shaping us into complete individuals. People who perceive failures, pain, and struggles as learning experiences are the ones who ultimately succeed.

- The way we perceive things influences how we interpret them

- When we recognize situations with a positive mindset, they appear positive

- When we approach them with negativity, they seem negative

- Therefore, our perspective is of utmost importance

Assuming is not life; Adjusting is life.

LIFE IS A SET OF ADJUSTMENTS.

- Adaptability has the power to change our lives.

- We must learn to adjust with our parents, siblings, relatives, friends, colleagues, fellow citizens, countrymen, and even people around the world.

- When we let go of pretence, ego, hatred, and unnecessary comparisons, adjusting becomes easier.

- Empathy, gratitude, forgiveness, humility, patience, and a broad mindset strengthen our ability to adjust.

- Loneliness and social isolation are said to be as harmful to health as smoking 15 cigarettes a day. They increase the risk of death by 29%. However, solitude, when used constructively, can create opportunities for success.

- Don't spend your days worrying about what others think of you.

- Be curious about yourself, cultivate mindfulness.

- Your problems are not bigger than you.

- Don't discuss your problems with others

- only share moments of joy.

- If you carry problems in your head, they become a burden; If you step over them, they become stepping stones.

- A lamp is valued because it overcomes darkness;

- Life gains value when we rise above difficulties.

- Every pain teaches a lesson.

- Every challenge shapes us.

"Do not pull others down—lift them up instead"

— Jayaprakash Nagathihalli

10.

HABITS SHAPE OUR BEHAVIOUR

"We are what we repeatedly do. Excellence,

*therefore, is not an act, but a **Habit.**"*

— **Aristotle**

Understand Uniqueness.

Habits change our identity.

Good habits make others look at us in a totally different way. They can also earn us greater respect.

Start new habits!

It is best to cultivate good habits from childhood. However, if you make up your mind you can cultivate new habits at any age.

In his book *7 Habits of Highly Effective People*, **Stephen R. Covey** highlights the following key principles:

Be Proactive– Take initiative

Taking control of our own lives is essential. We must respect our choices and take responsibility for them

Begin with the End in Mind–Start with a clear vision

Keeping our goals in mind helps us stay focused and work towards them with clarity

Put First Things First–Prioritize what truly matters

Many distractions may arise, but setting priorities correctly makes our journey smoother

Think Win-Win– Always think of a Win–Win situation. Foster a mindset of mutual success

Always aim for solutions where everyone benefits, rather than a win-lose approach

5. SEEK FIRST TO UNDERSTAND, THEN TO BE UNDERSTOOD–Understand first, then explain to others

It is essential to thoroughly understand a situation before trying to explain it to someone else. Active and empathetic listening plays a key role in effective communication.

6. SYNERGIZE–Work together effectively

By understanding others' perspectives with an open mind and fostering creativity, any team can become stronger and more effective.

7. SHARPEN THE SAW–Keep improving yourself

Continuous learning and regular practice strengthen us. It is important to recognize the value of habits and progress while maintaining balance in the physical, mental, spiritual, and social aspects of life.

The choice of habits is ours:

1. Waking up early and sleeping early
2. Exercising regularly
3. Engaging in positive activities
4. Reading and writing
5. Listening and observing
6. Appreciating and congratulating others

7. Exchanging good wishes
8. Setting clear goals and working towards them

The Life-Changing MAGIC of Microgoals

Small changes can lead to big results in life. Start practicing good habits immediately and witness positive outcomes sooner.

Poverty vs. Wealth–How Habits Shape Us

Dan Lok explains how our habits determine where we end up in life. Here's a comparison between the habits of the poor and the wealthy:

The Poor	The Wealthy
Watch TV	Read Books
Earn Based on time	Earn based on results
Blame others for their situation	Take full responsibility for their condition
Focus on saving money	Focus on investing money
Believe they already know everything	Focus on continuous learning
Think money is the root cause of all problems	Believe poverty is the root cause of all problems

Rely on luck and lottery	Believe in proactive action

Time Management: The Power of a Schedule

A well-structured schedule helps in effective time management. From waking up in the morning to going to bed at night, maintaining discipline over daily activities allows us to stay productive. Avoid unnecessary distractions and focus on what truly matters.

Focus on Actions to Experience the change

When you concentrate entirely on your activities, you begin to understand the impact of flow. Prioritization and systematic execution lead to effortless progress. As you move forward, training itself becomes an experience.

Read the author's other book, **"Every Moment, an Experience"**, and make this life truly your own.

Sweat Hard: No Bloodshed

These words emphasize the importance of preparation. With thorough preparation, there is no need for bloodshed. Let's put in dedicated effort toward our goals—consistent hard work always yields results.

Use Objects; Love People

There is a fundamental difference between people and objects. People have life, emotions, and value, while objects are lifeless. Unfortunately, some have become so obsessed with material things that they have started loving them instead of valuing people. True fulfillment comes from loving and respecting people as fellow beings.

It is crucial to show respect. Today, people should learn to be more humane. This is the need of the hour.

Good Habits vs. Bad Habits

A **good habit** is one that benefits individuals and society, whereas habits that are detrimental to societal well-being are considered **bad habits**. However Based on location and environment classification between good and bad habits may vary. It is essential to eliminate bad habits.

Avoiding bad habits ensures both **physical and mental well-being**, leading to a peaceful family life.

Habits and Hobbies

Our hobbies can also turn into habits. Some good habits bring joy, just like hobbies do. The phrase **"Hobbies are the rubies in the garland of life"** highlights their significance. Hobbies and personal pursuits serve as a measure of how happy we are in life.

Self-Control

When we have control over our thoughts and habits, they do not become harmful to us. Instead, they lead to positive transformation. This control is what we call **self-discipline**.

Turning Actions into Habits

Our consistent actions should transform into habits. They must be practiced daily and become an integral part of our lives. Just like breathing is natural and effortless, our positive habits should become our second nature. Such habits give our personality a special identity.

Ships Are Not Meant to Stay in the Harbour

"Ships are safer at the harbour,

but they are not made for it."

"What is the use of merely sitting idle without walking the path?"

–Raghavanka

Never Trust Fear–It Doesn't Know Your Strength

Face your fears head-on. Public speaking training can help build confidence, and physical activities can enhance inner strength. Engaging in adventurous activities is a great way to push past fear. Only by confronting fears can you truly boost your self-confidence. Inspirational stories, books, and movies based on real-life biographies can leave a lasting impact on your mindset.

Overcome Fear

"Do not be afraid of anyone's words
Do not live like a person ruled by desires
Do not depend on others for your happiness
Never forget that your life belongs to you"

– Swami Vivekananda

Criticism Fades, But Actions Remain

"Only those who focus on even the smallest details can achieve greatness."

–Jayaprakash Nagathihalli

11.

INNERCISE for the Exercise of the Mind

"All power is within you.

You can do anything."

— **Swami Vivekananda**

Dr. B.R. Ambedkar states that the development of the mind should be the ultimate goal of human existence.

Kuvempu says:

"What does the science of any era say?

Is there any greater science than the voice of the heart?"

The call of the inner self reveals the truth to a person and plays a crucial role in shaping their personality.

A person with external courage thinks of quitting, whereas one with internal courage thinks of winning. The body is merely a tool for achievement, but the mind is an illusion. True achievers are those who master their minds. Through continuous inner exploration, the mind matures.

Hunger and Achievement

Almost everyone works to satisfy their physical hunger, but those who strive to quench their hunger for knowledge ultimately become achievers.

Ideas rule the world.

Yes, this statement has been proven for centuries. Governments have risen and fallen. Continue making efforts to enhance your thinking abilities.

No matter the ups and downs in life, thoughts remain the primary capital and true wealth.

Mind is like a parachute; it works only when it opens.

Many people keep their minds closed, preventing transformation. As stated in the Rigveda, "great thoughts lead the way for all."

"Let knowledge flow from all directions."

Let us acquire knowledge, use it, and achieve success.

MIND YOUR MIND; MIND WILL MIND YOU

If you pay attention to your mind, your mind will certainly pay attention to you.

"The mind is truly a spinning wheel of thoughts."

— B.A. Shankar

One can sincerely follow self-formed thoughts or discovered truths of life. When these ideas gain universal acceptance, it is called talent. The fascinating fact is that the thoughts that resonate with an individual's inner self often hold true for the world as well.

Conscious Mind

Being in an awakened state is called the conscious mind. When we stay aware and focus on present matters, we can fully utilize it. Instead of dwelling on the past, those who focus on their future goals and make continuous efforts to move forward are the wise ones.

Subconscious Mind

The subconscious mind is like a gold mine. It holds our knowledge, experiences, skills, memory bank, and past events—essentially, a vast treasure. The key to accessing this treasure is the conscious mind. If we eliminate unnecessary thoughts and gather meaningful experiences, an immense wealth of life remains stored within the subconscious mind, ready to reveal itself when needed.

Water is the softest substance, yet it can penetrate mountains and the earth.

This clearly demonstrates the principle that softness can surpass hardness.

SUPER CONSCIOUS MIND

The **Super Conscious Mind** is the highest form of awareness, granting us access to an extremely refined state of knowledge. It is often experienced by those who have control over their minds, possess intellectual depth, and have strong foresight. This is also known as the **6th Sense**.

Only those who deeply understand the power of the mind can perceive this state. In ancient times, sages who engaged in intense meditation were said to have attained it.

Practices like **meditation, concentration, deep focus on a single thought, and total immersion in a subject** create a powerful impact. The **Law of Attraction** also plays a role in this process, helping to form an aura around you.

When your **mental energy** aligns with the universe, the right situations and the right people will come into your life at the right time, offering support in the most suitable way. The more you believe, the more answers you will receive.

Benefits of Understanding Mental Power:

1. Overcoming doubts and fears
2. Gaining self-confidence
3. Avoiding unnecessary thoughts
4. Developing deep concentration
5. Enhancing creativity
6. Improving memory power
7. Cultivating a positive mindset

With great thoughts, you can achieve great goals,
- Solve problems
- Increase your enthusiasm for life.
- Have good experiences
- You can always be a cheerful person

Managing Mental Stress Keeps Diseases Away

Many doctors state that by managing mental stress, one can avoid over 20 **different illnesses**. As the saying goes, **"Prevention is better than cure."** It is always better to be cautious before diseases arise.

Create a **positive environment, build strong relationships, and maintain a good work-life balance** to ensure a healthy and happy life. Focus more on positive aspects of life.

Stay Away from Anger

Many **accidents and crimes** occur due to uncontrolled anger. An proverb says, *"A nose cut in haste will never grow back."*

Instead of reacting impulsively, focus on **responding thoughtfully**. If you wish to be recognized as a good person, keeping anger in check is crucial. Whenever extreme anger arises, **shift your attention to a productive habit or practice**. Sharing your thoughts with close ones can lighten your heart. Watching **cultural programs, music, dance, and theater** can also be uplifting.

Worry Less, Think More

There is only a slight difference between *worry* and *thinking*, but the impact is huge. Worrying brings no benefits, whereas **constructive thinking** helps in overcoming problems. If you focus on thoughtful solutions, worries will naturally fade away.

Think Big: Achieve Big

Jawaharlal Nehru once said, **"Having low aim is a crime."**

The Five Zones of Growth:

1. **Comfort Zone**
2. **Fear Zone**
3. **Learning Zone**

4. **Effort Zone.**
5. **Success Zone**

One must move step by step through these zones to reach success.

The Key Between Effort and Success: PATIENCE

"An attempt may be a failure, but failure should not be a failure of an attempt."

3C's Formula

A powerful principle suggested by the author:

COOL–Stay Calm

Just as a cold drink refreshes us in summer, cultivate a calm and composed mindset to handle situations effectively

BE CALM

Imagine yourself in the midst of a serene, undisturbed natural landscape. This is the state of **calmness** that we should cultivate within our minds.

BE COMFORTABLE

Develop a **balanced mindset**. Challenges, problems, pain, failures, and criticism should not break you. Even in adverse situations, stay composed and make rational decisions. Relax and remain at ease.

You Reap What You Sow

The seed you plant determines the tree that grows. Similarly, the thoughts you constantly nurture will shape your life. The more you focus on certain ideas, the more they swirl around us..

Just as stronger **roots lead to better fruits, consistent effort guarantees success**.

The Mind is Life's Compass

If you find life beautiful, it means your mind is in a beautiful state. Mental well-being matters more than external circumstances. Therefore, everyone should work on strengthening their mental resilience. As the saying goes, *"Your mind shapes your destiny."*

Break Free from Mental Poverty

Many people, despite having everything they need, constantly worry unnecessarily. **Be grateful for what you have.** If you fail to appreciate your blessings, you may unknowingly invite **artificial poverty**, which could eventually lead to real hardship. Stay aware and cultivate gratitude.

Quality of Thinking

The quality of your thinking shapes the quality of your choices and decisions.

Your choices and decisions determine your actions. Your actions lead to results.

Your results define the quality of your life.

Great things always begin from within. - Quality of Thinking

The quality of your thinking shapes the quality of your choices and decisions.

Your choices and decisions determine your actions. Your actions lead to results.

Your results define the quality of your life.

"Great things always begin from within."

- JIM KWIK

12.
BEING CREATIVE

The ability to generate new ideas or objects through imagination or skills is called creativity.

It is useful for problem-solving, communication with others, self-expression, and even entertaining others.

In 1926, Graham Wallas identified five stages of thought in his book *The Art of Thought*:

1. Preparation
2. Incubation
3. Illumination
4. Evaluation
5. Verification

Guilford identified five key elements of creativity:

1. Fluency
2. Flexibility
3. Originality
4. Awareness
5. Drive

Common barriers to creative thinking:

1. Distraction
2. Lack of Knowledge
3. Rigid Thinking
4. Perfectionism
5. Criticism

Key traits of creative individuals:

1. They are willing to take risks.
2. They have a resilient attitude toward failures.
3. They are willing to be different.
4. They have the ability to make spontaneous decisions.

The Invention of Footwear

There was once a king who ordered a **red carpet** to be laid everywhere he went so that his feet would not touch the ground. A wise man, understanding the king's intention, suggested that simply wearing footwear would achieve the same goal. This advice eventually led to the invention of shoes and slippers.

15 Habits to Enhance Intelligence

1. Exercise daily
2. Develop healthy eating habits
3. Get good sleep
4. Set goals and stay committed
5. Spend time with nature
6. Engage in mental activities
7. Practice meditation
8. Participate in creative activities
9. Engage in meaningful conversations
10. Learn a new language
11. Read books that interest you
12. Regularly assess your progress
13. Apply what you learn
14. Question everything
15. Strive to be smarter today than you were yesterday

Creative Personality

Creativity is a form of mental activity. The process of creativity happens internally in the minds of certain unique individuals.

The word **'Srujana'** (ಸೃಜನ) comes from Sanskrit. In Kannada, we use the same term as an equivalent to the English phrase **"""Creative People."""***Srujana* means creator, innovator, builder, imaginative thinker, people with constructive qualities, and talented individuals.

In childhood, the ability to create comes naturally. At that stage, our minds move freely and without restriction. However, as we grow up and are taught rules and regulations, our thinking becomes more confined and limited.

Nobel Prize-winning physician **Albert Szent-Györgyi** described creativity as the ability to recognize uniqueness.

The object or subject that is discovered is something everyone has seen and thought about.

However, there is always a thought about something that no one has ever seen. In many areas of our lives, the ability to create is what keeps us lively and enthusiastic. Creative individuals are intelligent, possess a free spirit, and have an interest in every subject. They prove that their abilities are useful in specific fields.

Creativity develops through the reactions of a person" thoughts. It also has social and cultural connections. Not everyone possesses a creative personality—it is found only in a few exceptional individuals. Generally, creative people engage in self-reflection, deep concentration, and contemplation, allowing them to make unique contributions to society.

In one way or another, we all exhibit creativity in our daily lives. Homemakers, decorators, teachers, and even gardeners express creativity in their work. Creativity begins at home and continues throughout life.

Creativity in Artists

Since artists possess creative talent, they develop self-confidence and a sense of satisfaction in their work. American psychologist Gilford has identified six types of abilities that an artist demonstrates in their work.

They are:

1. Simple thinking
2. Explaining through comparison
3. Expressing
4. Establishing a connection between one object and another
5. Versatile composition or the beginning of innovation
6. Giving an artistic form to one"s desires or aspirations

"hose who put in extreme effort to do the

right work always seem a little crazy."

— **Stephen King**

13.
Be a New "You"

Every new day begins with fresh expectations. However, not all of them may come true. But each day always ends with a new experience.

Senaka

Newness–Innovation–Novelty should be woven into our lives.
Without them, life becomes dull and monotonous.

New Year–Ugadi

Just as we celebrate the New Year, we should celebrate each day of our lives.

The lyrics from the movie *Kulavadhu* express this beautifully:

*"Though ages pass, Ugadi returns again,
The new year brings new joy and freshness."*

Similarly, the song from *Hosa Belaku* offers inspiration:

*"The door is open, O guest, come in,
With the fresh breeze of new light,
Come, bring a new life."*

*"Whichever form you arrive in, it's fine,
Whatever attire you wear, it's fine,
Come with the kindness of the sun,
Come like the soft glow of the moon."*

The Importance of One Individual

An unforgettable incident from Mahatma Gandhi's life in South Africa left a lasting impact.

Through truth, non-violence, and Satyagraha, he showed the world that battles can be fought without violence.

Instead of asking, *"What can I do?"*, strive to be the spark that ignites the change you wish to see in society.

Sir M. Visvesvaraya's Extraordinary Life

Within his 100-year lifespan, he achieved what an ordinary person might take 2,000 years to accomplish. Anyone who observes Visvesvaraya's achievements would never question whether a single person can make such a difference.

Swami Vivekananda

He made the entire world turn its attention to India's culture and heritage.

Swami Vivekananda is synonymous with self-confidence. Pay attention to and follow his teachings.

Read the book "Saadhakara Chandana", where the author has documented interviews with 16 achievers. Their experiences will serve as guiding lights for you.

A Single Drop of Polio Vaccine

By administering just one drop of the polio vaccine to children, the disease was successfully eradicated.

1% Marks Can Change a Future

There are instances where a mere 1% difference in marks has completely altered a person's future.

Competitive Exams

For those appearing in competitive exams, the significance of 1% is well understood—even a small margin can change the results entirely.

1% Club

Let 99% of people be however they may—but be a part of the 1% achievers' club.

Establish yourself as an expert in your field, and take charge of its development through innovative and proactive efforts.

The Power of 1 Degree

- Airplane Navigation

A 1-degree deviation in an airplane's course can cause it to land in an entirely different destination than intended.

- The Unique Property of Water

Water heats up at 211°F, but at 212°F, it boils—this single-degree difference creates the steam that powers massive locomotives. A small change can have a significant impact.

The Power of 1 Second

- Olympic Medals

In athletics, a fraction of a second can be the difference between winning and losing a medal.

- Motor Racing

In car races, a difference of mere seconds can determine losses or gains worth millions.

Time is like the waves that hit the shore every day—the waves are new, but the water remains the same.

Just like that, keep reinventing yourself and presenting your personality in new ways.

"You define the moment; don't let the moment define you."

EXTRA Effort

Observe that those who put in extra effort always achieve greater growth and success.

Ordinary–Extraordinary

Just adding the word "extra" to *ordinary* makes it *extraordinary*. Similarly, a little extra effort can make a significant impact.

Unleashing Potential

Continuous effort helps uncover the hidden potential within us.

"Attempt may be a failure, but there should not be a failure of an attempt."

"Just as breath enters a man every moment, giving him new life,

The divine truth renews him and inspires him to bring newness to the world.

Only by sharing this renewal with the world does one truly fulfill life's purpose."

— **Mankuthimma**

Just as breath enters our body and brings freshness with every inhale, the divine essence enters a human, renewing him from within and inspiring him to work towards bringing newness to the world.

This deep connection between the divine and humans remains eternal.

Renowned poet **D. V. Gundappa** beautifully expresses this thought in *Mankuthimmana Kagga*.

"Life is in newness; decay leads to death.
Every day flourishes with fresh energy.

A smile, a word, a gesture, a glance — All bring charm when they are ever-renewing."

— **Mankuthimma**

There should always be novelty; that is life. Let the old fade away—let it go.

For vitality to emerge every day with freshness, if excellence spreads through words, actions, and appearance, life becomes beautiful.

To become a new person, certain aspects must be observed and understood.

Let's move towards success—come along:

1. From Indiscipline To Discipline

2. From Questions To Answers

3. From Comfort Zone To Effort Zone

4. From Uselessness To Usefulness

5. From Powerless To Powerfulness

6. From Dreams To Goals

7. From Preparation To Success

8. From Worries To Constructive Thoughts

9. From Spectator To Player

10. From Vagueness To Clarity

11. From Lack Of Knowledge To Great Knowledge

12. From Pain To Pleasure

32. Wander To Wonder-Struck

33. Ordinary To Extraordinary

34. Love To God

35. Ego To Proudness

36. Transformation To Achiever

For more information, read the book: Transform Your Life Instantly-

The book can be purchased from www.amazon.in

If you incorporate even a few of these aspects into your life, success is guaranteed. You will become a catalyst for transformation.

New freshness
New path
New joy
New enthusiasm
New hope
New excitement
New energy
New thinking
New energy,
New emotions,
New confidence.
May every new day be yours!

In life, any task that does not challenge us cannot change us.

"No matter how big the vessel is,
It can only be filled drop by drop."

— Gautama Buddha

14.
TIPS TO BE UNIQUE

"Every child is unique"

—**Aurobindo**

- Acceptance is the key to learning /
- Self-belief
- Confidence is essential for life. Faith is the foundation.

3. Adopt 3A's Formula:

- ALIVE
- ALERT
- ACTIVE

General knowledge should always be high.

1. **Don't React; Respond**

2. **Discipline In Behaviour And Expertise In Work Will Win Everyone's Heart.**

3. **Being In The Present**

4. **Readers Are Leaders**

5. **Involve To Evolve.**

6. **Empathise.**

7. **Be A Best Participant**

8. **Be A Continuous Learner**

9. **Be Assertive.**

10. **Acquire Leadership Qualities**

11. Be A Risk Taker

12. Don't Underestimate

You are a multi-talented individual. No one else can match the grandeur of your personality.

13. YUR DAILY ROUTINE 13. MATTERS About Your Routine

Keep this in mind.

14. FOCUS ON CONTINUOUS IMPROVEMENT

Life is a constant learning school. Learn lessons of joy from good people and lessons of pain from bad ones. True learning lies in digesting these lessons.

15. STRIKE A BALANCE IN LIFE- Achieve Control Over Life

The three essentials: **Family–Organisation–Society–** Maintain balance in all three aspects.

6 Aspects of Personality Development:

1. Physical
2. Mental
3. Intellectual
4. Emotional
5. Spiritual
6. Financial

Regularly assess these six aspects of life. Correct any imbalances and cultivate a broad mindset

16. WHAT NEXT? Now and then ask yourself, "What's Next?"

Even a small light of optimism can brighten the greatest darkness in life. With this perspective, we must always think ahead about the future.

17. DISCIPLINE MATTERS- If You Have Dedication, You Win; If Not, You Fall

"A prayer without devotion

Is like a letter without a stamp."

— Hiremagaluru Kannan

Determination is not just about getting what we want; It is also about earning recognition from those who once rejected us.

OPEN YOUR "EYE"& CLOSE YOUR "I"

"Be the change you wish to see."

— Mahatma Gandhi

15.
JP'S SUCCESS FORMULA

Based on my 25 years of training experience, we felt the need to provide readers a success formula. I felt the need to provide a successful formula to readers.

99% of our formula will make you an achiever.

If you need direct guidance, contact our office.

1. INFORMATION

Information is essential for the study of any subject.
The Information Age
The present era is recognized as the Information Age.
Information Technology has created a revolutionary environment today. Bengaluru is known as the Silicon Valley of India and also as IT City. Such is the value of technology based on information.
In our lives, information is recognized as fundamental knowledge. There is a saying, "Knowledge is power." Society respects those who acquire and present knowledge, whether they are scholars, poets, speakers, singers, or playwrights.

There is a demand for organized knowledge, and those engaged in such pursuits are also honoured.

2. VISUALISATION

Imagination is the source of creation, (Creation emerges form the Imagination) you imagine what you want.

"You create what you imagine."

— George Bernard Shaw

1. This is the process of giving shape to any kind of future idea. It is a valuable activity for both immediate needs and long-term visionary plans
2. An architect wishes to clearly define a building's structure through a blueprint. A visionary leader plans for the country's progress 50 years ahead

A person plans how he wants his life to be. Young men and women visualize the person they wish to marry.

Everyone dreams about what they want to achieve in life, and visualization has the power to turn those dreams into reality. That's why mentors like us suggest creating a **VISION BOARD** and placing it in a spot where you can see it daily. This has a surprisingly powerful impact. Since we see it every day, these thoughts remain active in our subconscious mind, guiding us toward our goals.

"Imagination takes us to a world that doesn't yet exist. Without imagination, reaching such a world is impossible."

— Aristotle

3. Motivation

Just as eating food daily is essential, staying motivated every day is equally important. A motivated state of mind keeps us highly alert and focused.

Author Jayaprakash Nagathihalli, through his Transformation Unlimited YouTube channel, provides inspirational videos to society. Subscribe and watch these videos regularly.

All the books written by the author are centered around motivation. Read these books:

1. Nudigannadi (The Mirror of Words)
2. Solugalige Anjadiri (Do Not Fear Failures)
3. Keelarime Enu? Eke? Hege? (What is Inferiority? Why? How?)
4. Experience Every Moment
5. Awareness of Turns in Life
6. Employment Skills
7. The Fragrance of Achievers

Books, videos, biographies, situations, stories, and wise thoughts can serve as sources of inspiration for you. Strive to be a source of motivation for others. As you do, the inspirational aspects within you will grow. Through speeches, training, and guidance, the authors aim to inspire themselves using their own experiences.

4. Communication

The three key aspects of communication skills—speaking, writing, and body language—are discussed.

The Art of Speaking

This is one of the unique traits of humans. Speech is considered as precious as a gem, as divine as the Jyotirlinga, and as powerful as all-encompassing armour.

Masti Venkatesha Iyengar said, "Words should unite hearts, not break them."

Adikavi Pampa stated, "Speak words that are kind, measured, and gentle."

Basavanna remarked, "Words should be like a string of pearls."

Sarvajna observed, "Laughter comes from words, enmity arises from words, wealth is gained through words—words are like precious jewels in this world."

There are many proverbs that emphasize the importance of speech:

"A person who knows how to speak has no quarrels; a person who knows how to eat has no illnesses."

"Words can ruin a household, just as a small hole can ruin an oven."

Once, when I requested Dr. Master Hirannayya to write a foreword for the book *Nudigannadi* (Mirror of Words), he responded, "If you raise a dog, it will guard the house; if you train your tongue, it will protect your lineage."

I often recall the words that were spoken. The book *Nudigannadi* serves as a guiding light for the art of effective speech.

"It is reasonable to remain silent when on should speak,

just as, it is unreasonable to speak when one

should remain silent."

–Jayaprakash Nagathihalli

Writing

The saying ***"The pen is mightier than the sword"*** is well known.

Students demonstrate their learning through writing in exams. Researchers state that handwriting helps information register directly in our brains. Beautiful handwriting may even fetch higher marks. While spoken words may vanish into thin air, writing remains as a permanent record. That is why even in court, written documentation is given higher importance.

Writing has been respected in all eras. Even after their death, poets, literary figures, and writers live on through their books. It is said that a writer's soul is hidden within their works.

Therefore, record your voice through writing—writers hold a unique place in our society.

Handwriting styles have gained diverse recognition across different languages. The field of graphology, which identifies personality traits through handwriting, is gaining popularity. It is believed that practicing writing with both hands can improve memory. Content writing is in high demand, and many writers are excelling on online platforms. Writing supports both profession and passion. Start writing and continue consistently—your writing can shape your destiny.

Body Language

Body language holds a unique place in communication skills. Those who understand its importance have no doubt about becoming successful individuals.

Posture and gestures convey our emotions to others. Our clothing, facial expressions, smile, and gaze communicate who we are. The more natural your body language, the more graceful you appear.

5. Transformation

"Change is the law of the universe," said Lord Krishna. A change that happens on its own is simply a shift, but a change we bring about through effort is transformation. This is the fundamental difference between animals and humans. However, despite transformations, it is ironic that humans sometimes exhibit beastly behaviour.

If we accept our current situation and strive towards the one we desire, anyone can undergo transformation. Sometimes, circumstances, situations, failures, betrayals, and pains can also become platforms for change.

The robber Valmiki became a sage. The fierce Ashoka became a messenger of peace. The incident on a train in South Africa compelled Gandhi to plunge into the fight for independence.

Gandhi said, ***"Be the change you wish to see."*** Instead of sitting and complaining about others, let us take the initiative ourselves. That positive change will be the foundation for transformation

Progress is Impossible Without Change

George Bernard Shaw

6. Implementation

We come across many intelligent people, but not all of them are achievers. The primary reason for this is that they do not apply what they have learned to their lives. As a result, they do not receive the benefits they deserve.

Many learnings become habits through consistent practice. By incorporating them into our daily lives and moving forward with them, we can truly live by the saying: *"Actions speak louder than words."*

7. *Gratification & Satisfaction*

If you follow all six aspects, true satisfaction will be yours.

1. Cherish the small joys in life
2. Be as cheerful as a child
3. Be a role model for others
4. Lead a simple life with noble thoughts
5. Connect with nature
6. Be socially responsible
7. Embrace the spirit of giving and generosity
8. Be a good person and always do good
9. A broad mindset makes you compassionate
10. Love others and allow yourself to be loved
11. Stay away from jealousy
12. Always stay happy

May you focus on achieving great results instead of making excuses. Wishing you a fulfilling path towards satisfaction.

In our Personality Transformation Camps, detailed training is provided on these seven aspects.

WINNERS NEVER QUIT, QUITTERS NEVER WIN.

16.

IMPLEMENTATION OF ACTIVITIES

Activities turn into guiding lights. There is greater clarity about the things you already know.

If you positively interpret the activities suggested in this book, your life will undergo the change. Your perspective on life will shift. Recognize a transformed individual within yourself.

WRITE YOUR OWN BOOK
Prepare an Index

1. If you were to write your autobiography, list the topics that would be in its index.

2. What words would you like on your gravestone?

3. Take a SELFIE with a smile, then take another photo without a smile. Compare them and write about your experience.

4. List your best qualities that make you worthy of being called a beautiful person.

5. What is your favourite book? Why do you like it?

6. Who is your favourite person? Why?

7. Which famous personality do you admire? Why?

8. Write an essay on the topic: "Who am I?"

9. List your new resolutions.

10. Create positive affirmations that you need in your life, print them, and place them in a suitable spot.

11. Identify and list people whom you wish to appreciate. Call them today, congratulate them, and send them good wishes.

12. Make a list of people to whom you owe gratitude. Find a way to express your thankfulness to them.

13. Prepare a checklist of your daily tasks.

14. Every night before sleeping, reflect on the beautiful moments of the day. Finally, contemplate the things that couldn't be accomplished—answers will become clear.

15. Read the biographies of achievers in the field you aspire to. Watch videos available about them.

16. Watch movies that portray successful individuals.

17. Some of the greatest movies in the world convey powerful messages. Watch selected films that offer meaningful insights.

18. Actively participate in social media networks.

19. Network is Net Worth—Stay connected with all the people you know by creating WhatsApp or Telegram groups and maintaining continuous communication.
20. Lead by Example—Become a role model for others.

*"It is not enough to achieve progress,
achieving excellence should be the goal of humans."*

— K.S. Nisar Ahmed

17.

GREAT THINKERS ON UNIQUENESS

"Your growth stops when you fail to understand the difference between virtues and vices."

— Gandhiji

"Personality is the seed mantra of a new era of success."

— Rama Shree Mugali

"I speak gracefully in simple words so that everyone understands clearly, without any flaws, what I have heard from others."

— Sanchi Honnamma

"If someone treats you badly, first try love. If that doesn't work, try compassion. If that too fails, maintain distance."

— Sadhguru

Life is neither a beautiful dream nor just a bitter neem; it is a mix of neem and jaggery. Some bitterness, some sweetness, a little laughter, a few tears, a little anger, and a little agony. You must swallow it all with a smile, turning pain into joy.

— Nadigeri Krishnarayaru

Work hard, work tirelessly, work more. Let there be effort in your work, discipline in your routine, a goal in your vision, discernment in your actions, and efficiency in your execution.

— Sir M. Visvesvaraya

"Stay away from those who discourage your ambitions. Only truly great people will inspire you to believe that you, too, can be great."

— Mark Twain

"If your determination to succeed is strong, failure will never hold you back."

"When talent is combined with scientific knowledge, it is like setting a diamond in gold."

— Dr. A.P.J. Abdul Kalam

Whatever people do in this world, they do it with hope.

— Martin Luther King Jr.

A successful person is one who builds a strong foundation
with the bricks others throw at him.

— David Brinkley

I do not consider mistakes as failures. They are simply
opportunities to find out what does not work.

— Thomas Alva Edison

Never try to defeat people, just win their hearts.

— Buddha

18.

CELEBRATE LIFE

"Brighten the corner where you are" –Ogdan

Bonnie Ware conducted research by interviewing people who were nearing the end of their lives. The key responses given by such individuals were:

"It would have been better if I had the courage to live my life the way I wanted."

"I shouldn't have worked so much throughout my life."

"It would have been better if I had the courage to express my feelings."

"I wish I had stayed in touch with all my childhood friends."
"I could have been happier."

Observing these responses, one important realization is that we should not reach a point where we say the same things. The best remedy for this is to celebrate each day like a festival. The more we celebrate, the more reasons for celebration become visible. Every day should be considered a lucky day. Ultimately, the choice to live this way is ours.

Every Day is a Celebration

Here are a few lines from the famous poem **"Nityotsava"** by poet **Nisar Ahmed**:

In the golden light of Jog Falls,
In the shimmering waves of the Tunga river,
In the towering peaks of the iron-clad Sahyadris,
In the ever-green forests,

Among the fragrant sandalwood trees — It's a celebration,
Mother, a never-ending celebration!
For you, Mother nature, an eternal celebration!

If we celebrate life every day like a festival, we develop a deep sense of gratitude towards it. It may not be possible to grasp the entirety of life all at once, but we can certainly make the most of each day. Only when we experience every moment fully can we truly savour the essence of life.

A river has countless feet—it continues its journey every second. Only by moving forward relentlessly can avoid stagnation. Similarly, if a person makes use of every moment with dedication and purpose, only then does their identity and existence find true meaning.

If every individual considers each day as new and fresh, life itself becomes a celebration. Enthusiasm sparks within, keeping the spirit young forever. Youthfulness takes root in the heart, and one shines with vitality. By embracing generosity while striving for progress, and by spreading love, one reaches the peak of happiness.

Every sunrise marks the beginning of a new chapter in life. The past is gone, the future is yet to come, how will the future be? What will it bring? We don't know. That's why the present is all we truly have. Our actions must align with the **"now."**What time gives us depends on what we give to time.

May the enthusiasm for life be yours!

1. Overflow like a fountain
2. Be like the air inside a balloon—light and full of energy
3. Let liveliness be yours!

Life is Yours

Many people live for others, while some spend their lives following others' directions. But this is **your** life—live it for yourself. I feel strongly toconvey the message that life truly belongs to those who claim it as their own. Only those who live this life as if it were their own have a purpose in life. They make life meaningful. It is our heartfelt wish that you become one among them.

Smile & Shine

There is a saying: **"A person with a cheerful face is always happy."** A simple smile helps us express joy effortlessly. Keep smiling always. Increase the moments of happiness in your life, and let humour be an integral part of it. Only when we spread joy to those around us we can truly be happy ourselves. Never forget to express gratitude for the support you receive from others.

To nurture and maintain relationships, one must understand that **no one is perfect, and no one is without flaws.**

Poet D. R. Bendre beautifully captured this in just three lines:

"Life is like water in the palm of a hand; experience it before it slips away."

Instead of saying, "Oh no, is it morning already?" we should wake up with wonder, thinking, "What a beautiful morning!"We shouldn't start the day with complaints. Every single day is a gift. We must realize that life is simply the journey between birth and death, and we should move forward in sync with time.

You Are the Hero of Your Life

1. Who are you?
2. What do you believe in?
3. What do you do?

If you can find answers to these questions, you can become the hero of your own life.

Reel vs. Real Hero

The heroes we see on screen (reel heroes) will not always come to our aid. Don't forget that you are the real hero and shine as the leader of your life.

Embrace Challenges

Happiness is not always found by searching for more, but by developing the ability to enjoy with less
"When a million things can bring you down, find one reason to keep you up."
Once you accept the truth that you cannot please everyone and start living for that both success and failure are temporary yourself, life becomes much more beautiful

Let the enthusiasm for life be yours. Begin celebrating each day as a festival from today—things will surely get better.

Difficult roads create skilled drivers. Rough waves create expert sailors. Challenging times build strong people.

Winners celebrate, while those who lose reflect and learn. The one who understands that **both success and failure are temporary** and finds joy in every single day.

> Life is a battle; but Look the battle is just a play!
> A picture game with no beginnings and endings.
> In this, defeats and victories are secondary
> It's important to play with ease.

> — **Mankuthimma** (D. V. Gundappa)

> Life is like a war; but it is a game of war
> A game of pictures with no beginnings and endings.
> where, defeats and victories are secondary
> It's important to play with ease

The secret to living longer and living well is simple: Eat half as much. Walk twice as much. Laugh three times as much. Love without limits.

Prepare Yourself for a Unique and Beautiful Life

1. Embrace and utilize modern technology wisely
2. Be your own competitor
3. Conquer yourself
4. Challenge yourself, not others
5. Question yourself from time to time
6. Stay focused on your efforts
7. Develop a magnetic personality
8. Cultivate the power to attract the best things in life
9. Live a life bigger than yourself

10. Fill your life with positive energy
11. Those who pay attention to small details become great individuals
12. Strength, enthusiasm, and dignity should define your journey

Even when the sandalwood tree is cut, it does not lose its fragrance.
Even when the elephant ages, it does not lose its majestic grace.
Even when sugarcane is crushed in a mill, it does not lose its sweetness.
Similarly, a person of good character does not abandon their virtues, even in adversity."

Prepare Yourself for a Beautiful Life Plan

1. Each day can be planned beautifully. Our actions must be thoughtfully executed, and planned tasks should be completed with focus and dedication. At the end of the day, we must evaluate whether we have used our time wisely
2. Prioritize your tasks and eliminate unnecessary distractions to make your work easier. Whatever you choose to do, do it with excellence and passion—true happiness is found in fully engaging with our activities
3. To become a truly unique individual, complete dedication must be a part of your character
4. If things don't happen as quickly as you expect, remember this:

5. It takes six months to build a Rolls-Royce, but only 13
    hours to make a Toyota. When you buy a vehicle, you
    receive a user manual. But when we are born, there is
    no guidebook for life. It is up to us to write our own

"If you just lie down, it's death.

If you just sit, it's disease.

If you just stand, it's a punishment.

If you keep walking, it's life.

'DON'T CRY, DO TRY'

Don't die with dreams; let us move on with memories."

19.

HAVE A MENTOR

"Mentoring is a brain to pick, an ear to listen

and a push in the right direction."

- John C. Crosby

MENTORING CHANGES THE WORLD

Mentoring will be a LAUNCHING PAD for your success. Even 10% of Growth will be recognised by others. Only 10% of the people are crafting a Life of CHOICE. These 10% people will have 10X growth. Don't just add years to your life; Add Life to your years. Even 10% of growth will be recognised by others.

Revolution has to be happened in the field of Self Transformation. Enjoy the process of pain to gain for yourself. Enjoy the rain & Enjoy the pain. Pain is the prize for yourself. Formal education will make you a LIVING & Self Education will make you a FORTUNE, You cannot have Social Transformation without individual Transformation. Ripple effect of learning will happen. Curiosity & Mentoring will change your life.

Separate yourself from the crowd, Learn to say NO when you want to say NO. Keep yourself busy with something or the other because, A BUSY PERSON NEVER HAS TIME TO BE UNHAPPY. Talk about your joys and see how wonderful life is. Work hard in SILENCE, let your SUCCESS be your NOISE.

Training & Development leads to constant LEARNING. Mentees will become CHANGE AGENTS. Customised Growth plan, that fits the individual & the mentor, Healing process will happen.

Follow your dreams and beware of pitfalls that life tries to hit us with. Life can be hard and it is not always far. But you have the potential to achieve great things. Things that are worth striving for. Not just for yourself but for society in general. Don't count upon yourself short. The sky is the limit.

Some succeed because they are destined to. But most succeed because they are determined to. The more you celebrate your life, the more there is to celebrate.

Everyday is a new challenge. In fact everyday is an opportunity to FLY HIGH. Until you spread your wings, you have no idea how high you can fly. Fly high, SKY IS LIMITLESS.

"A mentor is someone who sees more talent
& ability within you, than you see in yourself
and helps bring it out of you."

- Bob Proctor

EXPERT OPINIONS ON JAYAPRAKASH NAGATHIHALLI:

- **Justice Shivaraj V. Patil (Former Supreme Court Judge):**

  "A great speaker, writer, and personality development coach. True knowledge is not stored in the mind; it must be shared with society."

- **Dr. D.S. Vishwanath (Retd. IAS Officer):**

  "Among great names in personality development like Dale Carnegie, Anthony Robbins, and Stephen Covey, in Kannada, Jayaprakash Nagathihalli is a respected and commendable name."

- **G.S. Sridhar, Tumkur:**

  "After living with self-doubt for 38 years, J.P. Sir helped me overcome it in just one hour."

- **Dr. Amritaraj, Veterinary Officer, Harihara:**

  "J.P. Sir has the magical ability to correct and refine individuals."

- **Geetha, State President, Kannada Nadu Welfare Forum:**

  "He is the only person who answers our questions with clarity and wisdom."

- **Niranjan Gowda, Real Estate Entrepreneur:**

"Learning from a mentor like you is a blessing. Your guidance brings confidence, positivity, and prosperity."

MESSAGE FROM AN AWARDEE WHO HAS HONOURED BY QUEEN ELIZEBETH – II:

It is a pleasure to read your message. It tells us how hard you worked all these years to train the students to achieve their goals. I am one of your students.

The words you told I always remember when I faced the cameras in live Doordarshan interview. After our first discussion I asked you what is next hoping you may give me a big list of questions. You told me I will ask the same questions, answer as you did. It gave me confidence and now I can stand up and talk about my life experience on any platform. I am so gratetful for that .

Best Wishes,

Regards,

Dr. R.S. Suryanarayana Shetty

Doctor & a Judge

United Kingdom

FEEDBACK FROM THE FOLLOWER OF JAYAPRAKASH NAGATHIHALLI YOUTUBE CHANNEL

Firstly I saw your videos initially, they were very impressive and thought process is extra ordinary like out of the box thinking. I started watching all your videos some ignition started in me. I knew that you interviewed many great artists politicians businessmen and so many great personalities.There also your words and amount of knowledge you had was clearly visible. Your Chandana TV interviews and programs were Contentful perfect planned. I heard that you left job to serve society in the way of motivating people and making them find themselves.... recently your classes given in Sadhana academy youtube channel were really life transforming and the way you explained real life examples are just wah! sir..!! Really and many videos witnessing your friendliness and your interactions with many college students are great!! Whenever I see your videos I feel the real Life changer we are blessed that to in Kannada to have you.. now a days many people commit suicide due to lack of confidence ...but you are real hero filling lot of confidence and communication classes gave life to many people ..in finding best jobs in their career. your classes are golden classes sir..so many I can't explained your achievements in words. many classes I talked about you thanks for being a best motivational speaker real life guru..

Many students used to talk about your classes in Dharwad ...mainly for competitive field, for students from villages your are more important and valuable. Sure sir.

VITTAL TAPASI
Msc Agriculture in Genetics and Plant breeding
Research officer @ Corteva agriscience

Present address: Permanent address:
Hassan   KABBUR
                                    TQ- Chikkodi Ds; Belagavi
                                    591222

Author's Introduction

JAYAPRAKASH NAGATHIHALLI

- Transformation MENTOR
- International TRAINER
- Best Selling AUTHOR
- Social Media INFLUENCER

Email: smilingjp@gmail.com

Mobile: +91 9886081188

————————————

TRAINER

- International Trainer
- 30+ years of rich training experience
- Trained over 10 Lakhs people so far.
- Online: Silver, Gold, Diamond & Platinum Modules
- Offline: ONE DAY & THREE DAYS Workshops
- Associated with many reputed Educational Institutions, Government, Private, Corporate and NGO's .

————————————

SPECIALIZATION

Public Speaking
Communication / Life Skills
Personality Development etc.,
Customized Training Workshops

————————————

AUTHOR OF KANNADA BOOKS

1. Nudigannadi
2. Solugalige Anjadiri
3. Keelarime
4. Anukshana Anubhavisi
5. Udyoga Koushalyagalu
6. Tiruvugala Arivu
7. Ananyate Ariyiri
8. Sadhakara Chandana
9. Sahitya Chandana
10. Vyaktitva Chandana
11. Nirupane Rirupisi

12. Jeevanothsaha
13. Lifu Namdene
14. Vyaktitva Darpana
15. Vyaktitva Parivartane
16. Tarabetiya Takattu

—————————————

BOOKS IN ENGLISH LANGUAGE

1. Fear Not Failures
2. Inferiority Complex
3. Celebrate Every Moment
4. Transform Your Life Instantly
5. Unlock the Power of Uniqueness
6. Personality Mirror Transforms You

—————————————

VIDEOS ON

1. Humour
2. Examination
3. Failures to Success
4. Overcome Inferiority Complex
5. Be Happy
6. Be an Entrepreneur
7. Positive Attitude
8. Speech is Pearl
9. Enthusiasm
10. Turning Point
11. Unwanted
12. Art of Parenting

—————————————

AUDIOS ON

1. Personality Development
2. Time Management
3. Melody of Life
4. Self Confidence
5. Short Poems
6. Happy Married Life

[Audios & Videos produced by Nagamma Foundation (R)
- Please Call +91 934 125 9267 to purchase Soft Copies]
————————————

SOCIAL MEDIA INFLUENCER

YOUTUBE CHANNELS
- Jayaprakash Nagathihalli & Transformation Unlimited - Over
55,000 SUBSCRIBERS
————————————

CONTINUOUS MOTIVATION & TRANSFORMATION
THROUGH VARIOUS TOPICS.
Uploaded more than 5,000 Videos till date.
————————————

ENTREPRENEUR

Proprietor, Transformation Unlimited
————————————

PHILANTHROPIST

Founder, Nagamma Foundation ®
————————————

GRATITUDE FUNCTION
- Recognized more than 200 achievers till this year.

____

PAST EXPERIENCES – ORGANIZER

Overall organized more than 500 cultural and literary
programmes for the community.
1. President, Youth Writers & Artists Guild - 10 years.
2. President, Junior Chamber International &
Zone Officer for 1 + 2 years.
3. Indo-Soviet Cultural Society
4. Karnataka State Peace & Solidarity Organization
5. Program Committee Member, Bharatiya Vidya Bhavan

____

MEDIA TV HOST

Anchored programmes on Chandana TV, Bangalore
Doordarshan and interviewed more than 1,500 personalities for
Television.
News reader for 3 years.

____

RADIO

Presented more than 300 Radio programmes for Bangalore All
India Radio.
Presented the Talk Series 'Solugalige Anjadiri'[FEAR NOT
FAILURES] for Radio City FM.
Presented motivational series for Jnanavani FM.

____

STAGE SHOWS

Anchored more than 1,000 programmes.

———————————

ACTING

Acted in dramas, serials and movies.

———————————

KARATE

Trained by Dr.A.K. Atre, Former Principal,
Vijaya College, Black Belt Holder trained for 4 years.

———————————

WORKING TOWARDS PASSION

Gave up job in the Commercial Tax Department and became a
full-time trainer in 2008.

———————————

QUALIFICATION

Science - Arts - Commerce - Training.
1. B.Sc., from Bangalore University.
2. Masters Degree in Mass Communication & Journalism &
Diploma in Journalism
3. Diploma in Business Administration- 3 years
4. Excel Graduation from JCI University USA.

———————————

AWARDS

- Best District Youth Award
- Best Trainer of the year Award - Gurupuraskar
- Motivational Guru Award
- Super Achiever
- World Best Citizen Award
- Dr. Ambedkar Ratna Award
- Chanakya Award
- Sir M. Vishweshwaraiah Award
- Honoured by more than 1000 organizations
- Karnataka Rajyotsava Award by U CAN V CAN

———————————

VISION

- To train 2 million people.
- Be a Mentor for more achievers.
- To write more books.
- To inspire and transform through meaningful content on social media.
- Creating more Online Courses

———————————

Disclaimer

This book is written for teaching/ training purposes only. The readers are requested to note that the author does not render any legal, financial, medical, or professional advice. The content within this book has been derived from various sources. Please consult a licensed professional before attempting any techniques outlined in this book.

By reading this document, the reader agrees that under no circumstances the author is responsible for any direct or indirect losses incurred as a result of the use of the information contained within this document, including but not limited to errors, omissions, or inaccuracies.

Adherence to all applicable laws and regulations, including international, federal, state, and local governing professional licensing, business practices, advertising, and all other jurisdictions, is the sole responsibility of the purchaser or reader. Neither the author nor the publisher assumes any responsibility or liability whatsoever on behalf of the purchaser or reader of these materials. Any perceived slight of any individual or organization is purely unintentional.